CW01558757

528 741 96 4

Human Habitats

LIFE BY THE

SEA

By Holly Duhig

BookLife
PUBLISHING

©2019
BookLife Publishing Ltd.
King's Lynn
Norfolk PE30 4LS

ISBN: 978-1-78637-588-9

Written by:
Holly Duhig

Edited by:
Emilie Dufresne

Designed by:
Amy Li

All rights reserved.
Printed in Malaysia.

A catalogue record for this book is available from the British Library. All facts, statistics, web addresses and URLs in this book were verified as valid and accurate at time of writing. No responsibility for any changes to external websites or references can be accepted by either the author or publisher.

CONTENTS

Words that look like this can be found in the glossary on page 24.

HUMAN HABITATS

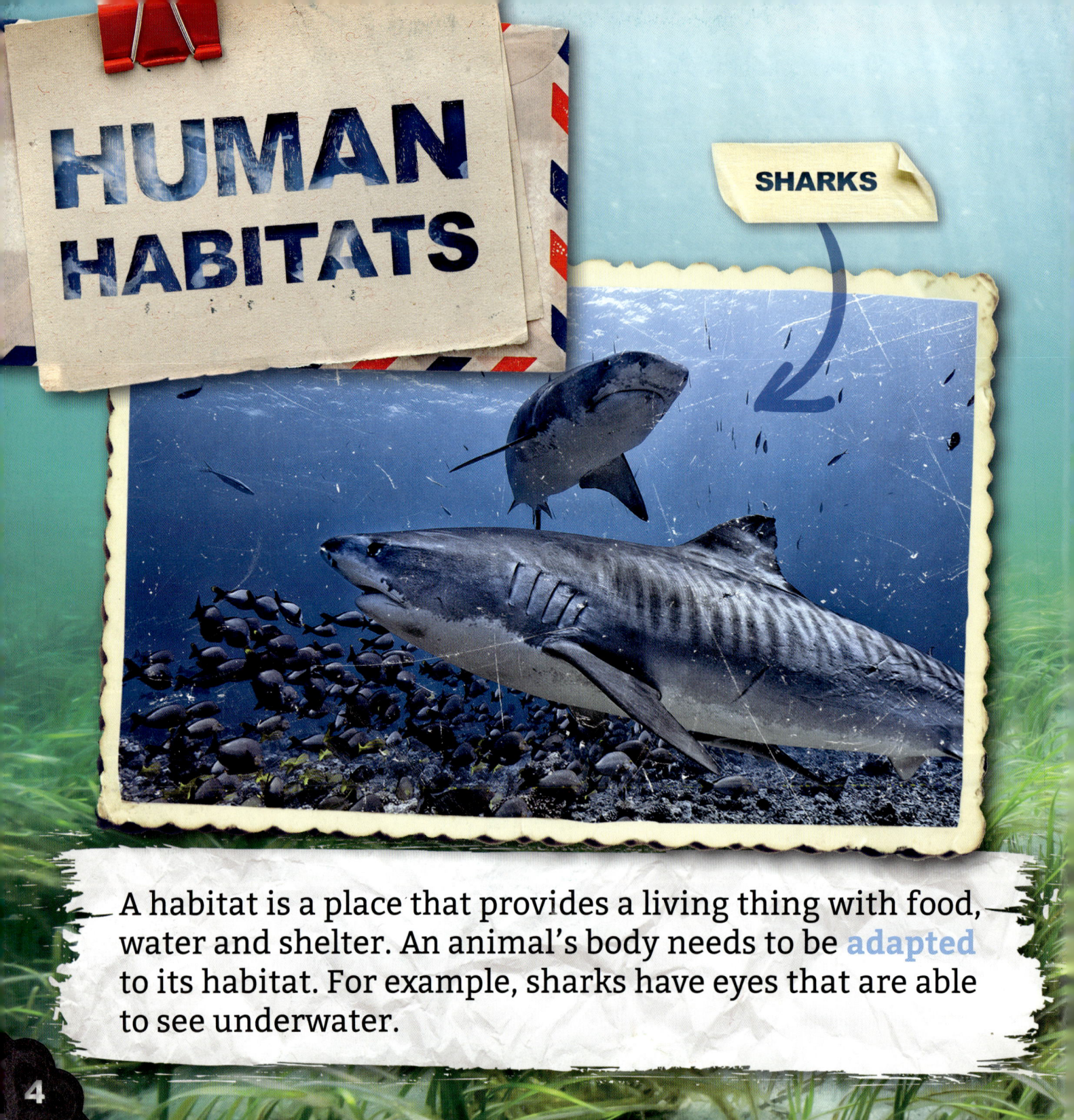

SHARKS

A habitat is a place that provides a living thing with food, water and shelter. An animal's body needs to be **adapted** to its habitat. For example, sharks have eyes that are able to see underwater.

Humans also have habitats. Unlike most animals, humans can survive in many different habitats and our bodies don't need to be adapted to them. Some human habitats are pretty extreme!

Humans don't have gills, but we can make snorkels!

OCEAN HABITATS

Where the land meets the sea is called the coast. Many people all over the world choose to live on the coast. Coasts in different countries can look very different to each other.

WHITE CLIFFS OF DOVER, ENGLAND

SEVEN MILE BEACH, GRAND CAYMAN ISLAND

Living near the ocean might sound like a lot of fun. Many people go to the coast for holidays. However, high tides, stormy seas and even tsunamis can make coastlines pretty extreme human habitats.

STORM WAVES

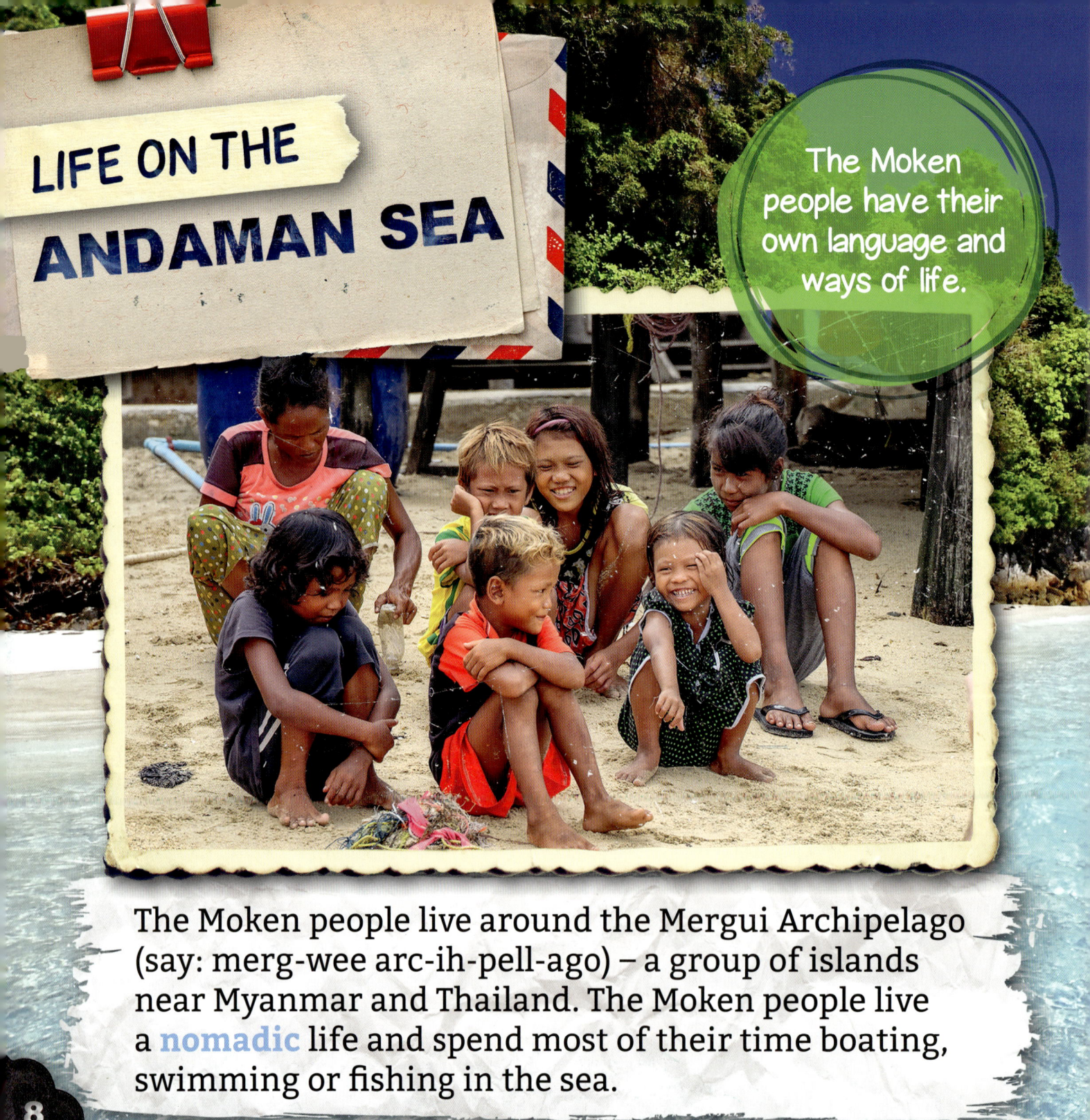

LIFE ON THE ANDAMAN SEA

The Moken people have their own language and ways of life.

The Moken people live around the Mergui Archipelago (say: merg-wee arc-ih-pell-ago) – a group of islands near Myanmar and Thailand. The Moken people live a **nomadic** life and spend most of their time boating, swimming or fishing in the sea.

Moken people spend much of their lives on houseboats called kabang that they use to move from island to island. Moken children are able to hold their breath underwater for much longer than other people and they can see clearly underwater.

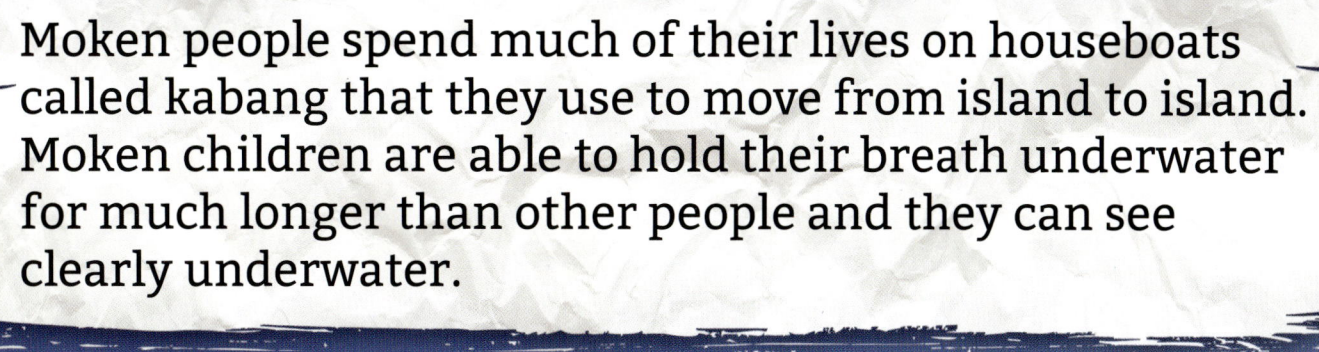

Moken adults can't see as clearly as the children can.

TSUNAMI SURVIVAL

In 2004, there was a huge tsunami in the Indian Ocean. Tsunamis are giant waves that can be caused by earthquakes on the ocean floor. The Moken people knew the tsunami was coming because they know their **environment** very well.

They noticed the animals were acting strangely. The dolphins were heading to deeper water and the land animals were heading to higher ground. The Moken people warned tourists and led them to higher ground too.

They saw the sea drawing away from the beach. This is what happens before a tsunami.

LIFE IN THE PACIFIC OCEAN

STILT HOUSE

Sama Dilaut people are also nomadic. Some live on and around a chain of islands in the Pacific Ocean near the Philippines. They live in houseboats and stilt houses built off the shore.

Some married couples live with their children on a houseboat. Other family members, such as grandparents, aunts and uncles, might live in a houseboat close by. Big families tend to travel together in a flotilla.

A flotilla is a small group of boats belonging to a larger fleet.

DIVING AND SURVIVING

This girl is searching for sea urchins.

The Sama Dilaut people are known for their diving abilities. They dive in order to hunt for fish underwater. The Sama Dilaut people can hold their breath for minutes at a time and can dive 20 metres underwater!

Diving far underwater puts a lot of **pressure** on your ears. For the Sama Dilaut children, their eardrums **rupture** at a young age which can make them hard of hearing in their adult lives.

LIFE ON AN OIL RIG

OIL RIG

Oil is used to **generate** electricity.

Oil rigs are large structures that are built far out in the ocean. They are places where people drill deep into the ocean floor in order to reach oil – an important source of energy.

To get to and from an oil rig, people must be transported by a helicopter.

The people on an oil rig don't just work there: they live there too. Usually, they will live on an oil rig for a couple of weeks before going home to their friends and family.

OUT AT SEA

Around 200 people might work on an oil rig at any one time. Some work day shifts and others work night shifts. The workers share rooms that look like cabins on a ship.

There is often a games room so people don't get bored.

THE WEATHER CAN BE VERY COLD OUT AT SEA!

Even when the sea is rough and the weather is stormy, workers still have to do their jobs. They have to wear warm clothes, hard hats and safety goggles.

LIFE ON THE
COAST

Tidal defences, like this one, direct waves back towards the sea.

Many people live on the coast of their country. Living by the sea means you get to spend a lot of time at the seaside. However, it is very important to stay safe at the beach.

It is important to know when the tide comes in and goes out. When the tide is 'high', the sea comes towards the land. It might even cover the whole beach.

TIDE TABLES

NORTHUMBERLAND COUNTY COUNCIL

TIDE TABLES TELL YOU WHEN THE TIDE IS GOING TO BE HIGH.

A FLOODED PIER AT HIGH TIDE

Strong waves and high tides can slowly wear away cliffs and beaches. This is called coastal erosion. Houses that were built on the tops of cliffs might eventually fall into the sea if the cliff erodes enough.

In Happisburgh, UK, coastal erosion caused these houses to start falling into the sea.

Can you name five things you might take with you on a beach holiday?

Many people make the ocean or the coast their human habitat. Some people live on the coast and some people go there on their holidays.

GLOSSARY

ADAPTED	changed over time to suit the environment
ENVIRONMENT	the natural world
FLEET	a large group of boats or ships
GENERATE	to create, produce or make
GILLS	the organs that some animals use to breathe underwater
NOMADIC	not living in one permanent place
PRESSURE	a force exerted on an object by something pressing against it
RUPTURE	break or burst suddenly
TOURISTS	people who are visiting a place for pleasure
TSUNAMIS	very large waves usually caused by an earthquake

INDEX